NIGHT SONGS

by Anne Miranda

BRADBURY PRESS · NEW YORK

Maxwell Macmillan Canada · Toronto
Maxwell Macmillan International
New York · Oxford · Singapore · Sydney

Bradbury Press
Macmillan Publishing Company
866 Third Avenue
New York, NY 10022

Maxwell Macmillan Canada, Inc.
1200 Eglinton Avenue East
Suite 200
Don Mills, Ontario M3C 3N1

Macmillan Publishing Company is part of the Maxwell
Communication Group of Companies.

First American edition
Printed and bound in Hong Kong by South China
Printing Company (1988) Ltd.
10 9 8 7 6 5 4 3 2 1

The text of this book is set in 20 point Goudy Oldstyle.
Book design by Julie Quan

ABOUT THE ART: The illustrations for Night Songs are cut-paper
collages. The paper was first textured with ink. Then shapes were cut
and glued to create the scenes.

LIBRARY OF CONGRESS CATALOGING-IN-PUBLICATION DATA

Miranda, Anne.
Night songs / by Anne Miranda.
p.   cm.
Summary: Describes the many different sounds of nighttime
ISBN 0-02-767250-6
[1. Night—Fiction. 2. Sound--Fiction.] I. Title.
PZ7.M6735Ni   1993
[E]—dc20   92-251

To Evan and Tyler

It's moontime.

Open the window and let the evening in.

Wrap yourself in warm

bedtime blankets.

Lie still.

Listen,

the night songs begin.

Cows huddle closely
in the grassy blackness
and low
as the crickets chirp
their scratchy meadow melody.

Ringed by reeds,
peepers peep.
Bullfrogs' tympany drums
croak and then repeat.
A springtime symphony
swells
in the fog-covered pond.

A stream rushes,
bubbling and babbling
while the mountain waits patiently
in stony silence
for the wind to whisper
a treetop serenade:
hush, h u s h, h u s h.

A storm comes up.
Windy fingers strum
endless rows of golden grain
like a prairie harp.
The rain beats a tinny tune:
pit, pat, pitter, pat,
against an empty silo.

A screech owl hoots
and swoops in feathered flight.
Other creatures of the night awake
and scurry,
chatter,
claw,
and squeak
deep in the forest.

The city sings its restless song
of cars and buses and trains and planes
and people—
a raucous tune.
The city doesn't sleep,
but simply closes its eyes
a bit,
to toss and turn
and snore.

Music rises from the desert,
hissing and sizzling like a pot on the boil.
A coyote howls—
two voices,
then three.
Their haunting lyrics echo in the canyon.

Waves hug the shore again and again,
smacking salty wet kisses in the sand.
Boats sway to the rhythm
of the rolling sea.
Their tingling bells
croon a love song
to gulls
listening in the harbor.

Coconut palms conduct
the island's solo.
Sweetly scented breezes beckon
to any passing near:
I'm here.
Come closer,
closer still.
Share
my twilight lullaby.

Sing, little one.

Hum along.

Close your eyes

and add your tiny harmony to the night songs.

Your warm breath sighing softly,

ever softly,

as you drift into dreams.